I met a girl among the hyacinths
with a bottle of dandelion wine on my hip.
our eyes locked and I breathed in
the nectar in the air, too potent
to drink and stare, too strong to swallow.

all was well

all was very well

as long as I looked in the right places.

Sleep Perchance © R. Wilson, 2022. All rights reserved.

No part of this book may be reproduced in any form or by any electronic or mechanical means, including information storage and retrieval systems, without permission in writing from the publisher, except by reviewers, who may quote brief passages in a review.

Paperback ISBN: 978-1-7775667-5-3

Published by Lucky Sprout Press.
www.luckysproutpress.com
Contact: info@luckysproutpress.com

Cover and book design by Offshoot Creative Consulting.

Cover image: *Still Life with Swan and Game before a Country Estate* by Jan Weenix, c. 1685. Public domain image provided by the National Gallery of Art, Washington DC.

Botanical illustrations from the Biodiversity Heritage Library.

Full-page paintings: *Flowers in a Basket and a Vase* by Jan Brueghel the Elder, 1615. Public domain image provided by the National Gallery of Art, Washington D.C.

Illustrations on pg 40, 64, 85, 90: adapted from illustrations by Giacomelli in *The Bird* by Jules Michelet, 1869.

Sleep Perchance

Poems and Illustrations
by Riva Wilson

LS
PRESS

"... and by a sleep to say we end
The heart-ache and the thousand natural shocks
That flesh is heir to, 'tis a consummation
Devoutly to be wish'd. To die, to sleep;
To sleep: perchance to dream: ay, there's the rub"

Hamlet, Act III, Scene I
William Shakespeare

Table of Contents

i   Introduction

Awake:

1   The Quick-to-Call
7   Inward Bound
9   Draught

Departure:

13   Ascend
16   Meeting
18   Attending
19   The Key
22   Can't Quite Remember
25   Two Days
26   Fly Bird
29   Too Beautiful
32   Needs Time
33   Shift
35   Ghost

Transformation:

43   I Want To Stay
45   Forget
46   A Prayer
49   Is She...?
51   Burdens
52   Return

54	Ungrateful
56	I Am So Afraid
57	Devotion
59	Rot
61	Tracks

Evolve:

67	Medicine
71	Unbutton
74	Cracked Foundation
75	The Thinking Place
77	The Long Sentence
78	Awakening
79	Indentured
86	Withdrawals

Exodus:

93	Maelstron
94	Burn The Witch
100	What Happens Next
102	Pocket
104	Renewal Season

Foreword

Sleep Perchance is the story of someone who is dealing with unsolvable problems: change, missed chances, inward and outward strife. The narrator finds a remedy in her own psyche; by diving inward to the realm of sleep, she is able to live a thousand lives where she can try and solve the problems that plague her outer world. However, the idylls of the dream world are not what they seem to be, and a new struggle emerges between what is perfect but fake and what is real and complex.

This journey is almost entirely fictional, with a few brief flashes of my own memories interjected. My original idea for the collection was to create a cottagecore wonderland where I could explore landscapes that were bursting with life and sapphic clutter. However, as I started to create these wordscapes, an underlying horror started to emerge behind it all. The idyllic scenes started to bleed with surrealism, and the edges of these spaces seemed to fade out into blank space. Instead of creating a snapshot of loveliness filled with flowers and gingham, I found that these things were instead decorations that covered a thin veneer over some very real anxieties, both personal and social.

In order to explore this idea further, I created a narrative with a very realistic foundation: the self-loathing and insecurities that come from failing a relationship and finding yourself unable to salvage it or turn back the clock. In this case, control becomes the ultimate goal: to be in full control of your self and the people around you, especially when they've caused you pain. The narrator of this story sinks into a dream world she controls where she can live out every perfect fantasy, until the dream gets out of hand and gains a sentience of its own. The helplessness that she felt in waking life is then mirrored in the dream world: she's become a supporting character in her life yet again. Eventually the truth of what she must do becomes clear. In a very kill-your-darlings way, she needs to wake up and come back to life.

Poetry was the perfect medium for this project, as the fractal nature of it complemented the amorphous structure of the dream world. The story starts off with more everyday language and imagery, as the narrator explores her current situation and reflects on the things that led to this point. She didn't take her relationship with the other woman seriously enough and assumed it would always be there waiting for her. When the other woman starts a new relationship with a man, the narrator struggles with the idea that she actually lost in this game of love. A hard reality to accept, to be sure.

Nobody wants to think of themselves as the villain of a story. But sometimes things happen that show us plainly how wrong we've been. Life gives us a mirror to see ourselves more clearly. That can be an impossible pill to swallow, as we have to put so much aside (like ego and our personal narratives) to accept this truth. Understandably, this can lead to a real mental crisis, which in turn can lead to so much escapism and denial.

My hope in writing this narrative is that you'll resonate with the emotional journey that unfolds across these pages. The story invokes everything from spiraling heartbreak to being drunk on love, until finally the narrator discovers that she has a choice: things don't have to stay the same, and she doesn't have to cling to old visions of the future. We can always choose to start writing a new story, to build a new world. Always.

See you in the garden,

Riva Wilson

Awake

forgiveness is a buffet

at a feast we throw

for all those we are eager

to continue loving

content to let ourselves

starve

The Quick-to-Call

in the busiest time of life
I was alone, pretty much,
and now a thousand miles away
my eyes find nothing but the sadness
in those photographs.

I sat there with the weight of loss on me,
the frantic plans and compromises.
I could go back to my suburban life
rent a four-bedroom home on five acres,
adopt a big white dog.

she was the pretty girl, so completely
taken care of, promised and accepting
the world. ah, a bird
pecking to get out of the pitcher
who simply would not fly
or twit.

a strange cage for a cageless thing
but with his usual iron grip
he forced her back by the beak.
a question. a response.

the quick-to-call won't help her. they're the quick-to-call
who see everything as smoke – steam, fog, breath.

I thought of going with pen and ink

seeking some permanent way to say my
objections, that though the case was closed
there was still a defender, once.

but the thing was, I was thinking so hard
I could hardly keep my eyes open.
sleeping was the cure for that.
it's part of nature to always think
of an action, but sometimes the fix
is in the stillness.

that's how I realized that
everything was changing
that there were problems
just as there always were
when we admitted
to growing up.

hadn't she always said
I was a fool to think that I
could feel her here?
the press against my chest
had started to lessen.
I'll tell you this much
I'm not human anymore.
her look of joy
as she carried me into her heart
as consolation only
means I'm no more.

and even still
before I knew it I lay
once again

with her resting on top of me.
what the hell had I done?
the next morning
she was gone before I woke.
I curled up alone
feeling that feeling again
one I nursed like a
raw and crusting wound
sick with some sort of
commonplace infection.
laughably common.

I didn't want to come back
but I had to, even though I would prefer
to stay on the run.
my runner's legs are what got us
into this mess, after all.
this time, I found an excuse
that would not be questioned and
I sat down and wrote.
staring at the words
I did not realize it was a letter
but I knew it was important
a severing
of self-preservation
my oxygen mask
before yours

you see, it's just a thing we do
now that we're *friends*.
I'll tell you how sorry I am.
for everything I did, I mean
well that's not quite true

mostly just for breaking our hearts
and never explaining why.
my not being there
and your depression

now that really was a crime

and in my selfish selfish ways
I label your recovery as revenge
breaking my heart twice

sometimes I wonder
what *happened* to him
to someone I only knew for
a few months. who I called
cruel names like
consolation and distraction.
he was here, but then he wasn't.
did he run away like the others?
I've seen him there with her but
that's not the man I remember.
he's not an elusive dreamer,
the kind you normally like
and I never thought to guard you
from shapeshifters
even when you were mine
to guard.

he told me we were real friends
once, standing around the bonfire
with cold beer while you went
inside to find his lighter
I told him I didn't believe it but

that's what you called it
friends.

we had a lot to talk about then.
he told me he was afraid
of being found out, but I
thought that was stupid.
he said he wanted to start
a new life, but that you
would be his priority.
I told him he could make it on his own
but I don't think he took it
to heart. he told me
he was sure he could make it
with just the two of you.

even in his dreams
you were always a set piece
never a participant
never with a line of
dialogue.

and now we're here
I barely understand it
you said you loved him but
you were lying
because everyone knows
that you're in love
        with

that time we were on the island
and he stood over as I lay
in the sand, as you threw yourself

into my arms
and he said he didn't believe
in our love, that it was just
an excuse
only we could see that dream

anyway.
I try not to think of
what could have been.

I write the letter
I put on the mask
I untether the rope
and let your ship
drift out
to different seas.

Inward Bound

I never found solace so instead
quietly I put together the pieces.
I told no one that
I had found any answers;
let alone that I had questions
to begin with.

I felt sick
putting on brown leather
shoes with the frustrating zip,
that yellow yellow nausea
putting one arm in, and then another
a thick layer of new flesh
painted over sweat-stained
purples and greens.

sick? no
it couldn't be
as simple as that.

but I had travel plans
places I was going
that my body could not follow
so that rotten thing
was tolerable
for now

a bomb had to be planted

there had to be another way
to get there
pardons had to be arranged
to help me escape

but coward is as coward does
and my better judgment forces down
the medicine, even though surrender
would be so easy
I could do it in my sleep

in my sleep

now, there's a thought

even if I couldn't get out
I could get in

and *in* was a road
I could walk a thousand times
in a single night

Draught

I closed my eyes
and hoped for the impossible
when I awoke

the skies
could be unfamiliar, the girl
could be someone else
entirely.

the only magic I could believe in
was the kind that didn't need you
to believe
the kind that plows forward
without regard for something as
unchangeable as
your faith in it

that's what I was looking for.
some great uncaring beast
to carry me along with it,
who would want me drenched
in numbness, the kind
that comes from the surrender
of your body
in between soft sheets
and darkness.

so I laid myself on the road

smothered my skin in honey
closed my eyes
and said
please

for a little while

let it all be different.

Departure

find and treasure some small place

meant for you to surrender

just soft enough to allow

hesitant longings to creep

up on little cat's feet

timid but finally able to

make themselves known

Ascend

before a darkened room
the curtain lifts (applause)
and there, a perfect rendition
of a newly minted summer night.

a safe forest with
a dozen tempting paths to follow

a belly that never hungers
but every bush an opportunity
to sup on heavy berries
never-staining and ever-sweet

never hungers but aches
for the glut of knowing.
the scent of wood smoke in the air
is a sign that time may be measured
in restful, motionless minutes.

the woods become the classroom.
there is a fat red deer,
a schoolmaster.

not everything in the wild is
kindly, but it is the wild.
it's full of delicious smells and
lonely sorrows
exciting

unending

three foxes run across a saffron field
a herd of blue whales slumbers
in the void below

the dark must wait
while the faintest light
starts the day that ends the day

a cottage, some rose bushes, spilling
lilies and leaves that shade the roof
flickering like a nightlight.
seven lamps, like a meadow
full of lightning bugs
are lit and waiting.

even if there was another
choice, I'd still
just let my magnetic legs
run me towards it
to a bed that needs a name
and someday a bride

but for now she's just
a bare bank of pink clouds
hanging between the kissing stars.
the sky almost looks like a naked woman
a mass of mosses

I don't know what it's called to have
a home at the edge of the world
a home that is for everyone, a wife,

a child, a friend
with the luxury of time

but first let my stomach
do its familiar routine
of clenching and twisting
to keep me still

for now I curl up on a hill
in the shadow of the moors
and weep for a place where
there is a story
and to be a part of it all

slumber with the blanket of moonlight
curled around me like a dog
keeping the three of us warm:
you, me, and the blue black sky.

Meeting

warm hands woke me
to the soft, ruffling touch
of the breeze.

I stumbled out to see
my bag tossed on the ground
clothes wet and muddy
being carried off by the
brisk wind.

naked, dirty, cold, but with
a knowing inside
I would find the part of the river
that runs through my veins
seared by the desire to stay
to listen
and make a home

I walked up to the cottage
my first time on flagstones so familiar
the door opened and

out came the lady of the night
of spring and bloom and death
on hands and knees and towering
high above me.

the one who opened my eyes

took my coat, placed it
on the wooden floor
mud and all

I heard the sound of a glass
being filled, shoes creaking
on the floor

my first kiss
of her lips
no need but to get inside
her pink mouth tasting
sweet, her eyes
impenetrable.

it was all I could do
no urge to fall
nowhere to hide
in the room of wood
the narrow spot where fear
and love are born

that night she turned
her back briefly
and I could hardly feel
the fog in my soul

only the flutter of her
hair, the bright red
of her eyes

my eternity my heart
my soul.

Attending

like coming home from a long journey
she settled me down in an old wicker chair
rubbed the soles of my feet with
lavender and vetiver
unpacked my bags and washed my linens
scrubbed the soil from the treads of my boots
lit incense
traced lines up and down my arms
plying me with sugared violets
I somehow remembered
her making in the spring.

I'm so sorry, I said, unable to help
the guilt. *I didn't come here
just for you to serve me
like this.*

she pitied me
with soft eyes
as you look at a child.

*how sick you must be
to feel sorry
over being cared for.*

The Key

on an ordinary day she brought
me a box in brown paper,
tied with a fir branch
knotted in the string. I hesitated
until she told me
that she'd been waiting
for the right moment
to deliver this - that it was
always mine, though I
would not remember.

in the box was a key
a map
and a bag of stones

in my soul it felt like
some sign of warning
and some morsel of temptation

I made up my mind right away
to go out and then back
to the glen, to the sea
so I took the map alone

in a trance I set out, bounding
running like an animal. I came back
the same way and a week later
sat under the thousand-year oak

in the village where we lived, feeling
the wind in my hair.

I had forgotten adventure.
she returned it like a lost ring
that rolled beneath the stove.

back home
I kissed her rosy cheeks
picked up the key from the floor
where it had fallen
and glared at the stones

heavy things
begging to be pocketed
to slow every step as I tried
to run madly

we gathered them up
together, put them in a thick
cloth sack and stowed them
in the back of the broom
cupboard.

she never said a word, only
helped me move the bucket
and the stepladder so I could hide
them properly.

a honeydew day followed, but
as I lay down to sleep I found
myself thinking that one of those stones
might bring me back

to that place I couldn't remember
anymore.

I never wanted stones
only maps and keys
and their revelations.

I always thought they would
come to me on the path
or in my dreams.

and if they did not
and all life could offer me
was stones, I'd put them
into my chest
and let that furnace
of deep deep passion
smelt them into iron
I might turn
into a key.

Can't Quite Remember

small house, small windows,
small doors with room for a body
filled with longing and lust
for the quiet. a taste of something
simple, something I once knew
in childhood, but do not know
and long to know again.

looking back I see
a human with a large heart
in a growing world.

the wind rustles through the trees
a raindrop pops on the ground and
I wonder:
where is the heart
in a city
where the sky is too far
beyond my reach?

Two Days

she gave me two days to think
about returning to that world
the fuzzy out-of-focus
place where I came from,
the womb of my troubles

a city filled with noise and a need
to show up, present myself as
something that fits nicely in
to a story where I am only
the chorus, if I audition
correctly.

two days.
I heard her at the end of my lullaby
the faint music of Debussy
strolling into the foggy
banks of my mind

I quickly wiped my eyes
strode into the quiet house
closing the door against the grumble
and clatter of the streets.
fastening the shutters from the
dust and shouting, the chaos
of the real world, I turned to attend
the shrieking kettle in my last
farewell.

Fly Bird

the night was berry dark
and the sheets twisted
around four ankles were
white with a field
of strawberries.

juice dribbling down and
sticky fingers. outside the window
the stars peered in to guard
the delicate blooming something
that was forming inside.

outside the strolling world
waited patiently. it knew my habit
of wandering as the sun slept
led by the map tattooed
across my chest in red ink.

*walk down the streets of spring
and take a road that is direct,
but watch the cat following on the wall
hunting for food.
stay on the path. he won't leave
and will only grow larger.*

the cat smells strawberries
on my breath and is waiting
for his chance.

don't move and I'll keep you safe
don't get curious and I won't get mad
close your eyes and you'll be safe
but who knows what lurks in the night

don't play with my tail or I will
claw out your eyes. hurry home
and I'll catch up soon. go before
the summer is over and you turn
into a goblin.

the steel within me refuses to
listen. I've danced this waltz
before, seen the shadows lurking
down every alley – but between
the choice of a gambler's walk
and conceding to their rule
I always roll the dice.

a pair of green eyes, filled
with mischief and a smile
that grows wider and wider
begs me to run away, just
a little chase. but the map
scalds its brand, demanding
to be acknowledged.

at the end of the road two boys
stand against a tomb while
a snake writhes around a spear.
the tomb is yours, the spear is his,
and the snake is but a piece of bait.

*shoo, bird, fly away or
he'll get to you. the birds
are scarce now, there is
no shelter. shoo, bird, fly
away or he'll get to you.*

in that night I realized
that though the paths are
endless, the journeys without
number, and the freedom
to choose unchallenged,
there are still dark things
waiting at the end of
certain roads.

sometimes it is better
to arrive home while
being chased than
to not arrive
at all.

Too Beautiful

her hair hung down over
a freckled shoulder, a soft
veil brushing down to rest
on the frill of her blouse
swaying little by little with
each stroke of her brush
completing another sweet
work we will tuck into
her folio.

I sat and watched her
work on the round
flower-bound window
she captured. was there
anything she did that wasn't
perfectly scripted?

a perfect character from
a perfect story. I hoped
it was a romance, a
dashing one with ships
and longing fulfilled.

but there were moments when
her eyes became vacant in
her perfectness. "I know
that girl – she's so beautiful,"
comes the voice from the

lane out the window
perpetually on display
a snow globe of a woman.

I watched her lips form
perfect human speech
with lines plucked
from a font.

she struggled to bring
her own beauty into
each day. there was no way
you couldn't see it.

yet here she was indeed
perfected, a creation
of a place trying to be
just what was needed to
be seen. when her voice
returned to life, words
what they wanted to be,
I smiled and bid her farewell
until dinner

(never once crossing
my mind that I too
only sat and stared until
the flakes settled
at the bottom)

something was wrong as
soon as I left the light of
the window. an errant wind

had me in its grasp, out
the door. it tugged and wrapped
until I was under a sky
so full it seemed
to float.

the light was always brightest here
when all the set pieces fell away
I felt an umbra all around
waiting to devour.

I was losing my way
thrashing against the sky
the light
but today I again freed
myself.

the world below, its voice
so vibrant but so weak
hanging there, like a
hurt pup, trying to speak
but lost in the crowd.

I dove back down
and bolded the lines around
the village, painted a
fresh wash of colour
across the gardens spilling
with pollen nectar ambrosia

I have always been
so much stronger
than my body, after all.

Needs Time

warm sunday morning
force feeding sticky dough
more flour, shaping and
rolling and smacking into
a round. I wiped my dirty
hands on the flour sack
towel, giving myself another
job once this was done.

I stared at my soon-to-be
loaf, wondering suddenly
why I had asked this simple
thing to take on the role of a symbol
of all my future happiness

an icon of a life of
production where I never
saw the result

it seemed to sit so deflated
on the wooden slab, unaware
of all its assigned expectations

give it time, I heard her
voice say more in memory
than not. *give it time and
somewhere warm
to rise.*

Shift

the first time I decided
to shift the narrative
between us, we were
lying in the meadow
breathing hard, having
finally caught the cat
who had leapt from
the window and given chase
for half an hour. she held
the escapee in the air
above her laughing
at his sour look and
I decided it was time
my lips bitten and fearful
took charge from my doubting
mind for just a hair's width
moment.

I kissed her with a
mewling passion that
threatened her control
of the situation and
of the cat

his ears tipped back and
his stare became hard
as he spilled into the
tall grass of the field

angry at my act
of violence

but she allowed my hold
on her, and I hoisted her
from the ground offering
no mercy to the cat
who ran off again for
the trees

her small arms
gave short distances
for that fast fall

Ghost

alone in the garden, I thought
about the heaviness in my body
borne from this knowledge I
just couldn't kill: that I must leave
eventually.

I did not want to dwell on
realities I refused to accept, and so
twisted my hands into the sky
branching and posing in the form
of the caribou, shaggy brown face
and soft eyes flickering
in the sun. I wished the shape
was real, more real than I could
conjure in this place. wished I could
grow warm with feeling, wished
I could simply stay.

as I walked across the tickling
grass I thought about the faceless
woman who lingered in the corners
of my memory – her name was
gone, but the anger remained.
I could name it now. the next
time I saw her, whoever she was,
I would turn her into a beast, devour
her, tear flesh off her bones
make her taste the pain I suffered

such was the justice of this world
where impulse was a higher power

in a field not so far away, two
elephants clashed together, their eyes
locked and their blows like punches
to the face, blow after blow
yet they never seemed to catch
the other. the war was unending and
they continued until
slaughter was the only thing remaining.

I strolled along the street to the
village lined with rock-trimmed gardens
housing curious summer flowers
only to stand before a lone building.
its tall silhouette, the wooden sign
swinging from its porch bearing golden
letters I could not read. a stain on the side
and the shutters hiding the windows
told a story familiar to all places
intentionally abandoned and intentionally
reclaimed.

I was staring at it with my hands
resting on my shoulders, trying to ease
the tension in my body. I turned to leave
but a shadow flickered, giving pause
to see a young woman in a white
faded dress with black pinstripes, her
face echoing my own: the exact same
shades of grey and brown where
I thought mine should be.

she watched me with a brow
that turned up as she spoke:
come here, can you hear me?

I did not like when my kingdom
misbehaved, serving up
things I had not ordered, but
this was becoming far too
frequent.

in answer I reached out with hands
meeting hers and closed our eyes
to focus on softening the intention
of this vision. my skin touched skin
surprising me. I needed to play
this one out until the end.

with interlocked fingers we ran
through the empty streets, taking no time
to conjure friendly faces peering
through the doorways. we ran until
we collapsed on the top of a hill, one
I'd found perfect for picnics with my
love. but now she was nowhere
to be seen, left behind in
our cottage, weaving her
enchantments for the evening
service.

tonight I would not attend, for here
the darkness began to embrace us.
as my companion folded her hands
upon her waist, we watched

the world from above. I found my voice
as she spoke and the words flowed
into me like a fountain. the light
sunk below the horizon and welled
up in my stomach. my voice came out
of her mouth, and so we spoke
together
about the darkness we did not
care to name.

it is a cold ocean in the summer
I think we are both seeking the
same thing, but I am the one who
sees it: the road
to the sun.

I woke up the next day weary
but elated, despite knowing that
the story was taking unauthorized
turns. I walked to my window
and caught sight of the pair
of conjoined twin mountains
that now looked so like the
ankh symbol
of the gods

sitting in the empty living room
I found a mirror and looked at
my body, learning that I am not
just a face. I touched the smooth
inclination of my neck and so
the discovery of my body continued.
I am a torso and legs, arms

and fists, hands and yes
even a face. I rubbed my
eyes and looked again, then
knowing what to do.

I lit a burner on the stove and watched
the flame ignite then poured in
the words to a song I had written
to the world a couple months prior.
as the fire played I sang it
taking one finger to stroke the smoke
in the air and watched it dissipate,
leaving greasy grey markings
across my flesh, a new map overlaid across
the old red scar.

I approached the pair
of twin mountains
the memory of my song
still stuck in my mouth
and I sang
hallelujah

Transformation

the stars are long familiar

with inconstant wishers

it is in their nature to forgive

the constantly rewritten vows

made upon them

I Want To Stay

I left the door ajar so silent footsteps
would be met with a silent exit as
I walked a little after midnight. I left
her sleeping, not meaning to keep
secrets, or so I told myself. I didn't
mean to sit beside the edge
of the pond longing for something
I could not describe, and feeling
the shame of it.

shouldn't it be enough?
crafting something perfect
and finding it lacking.
what's wrong with me?

and then that sweet face rose
from the water. I didn't mean
to go again, and again
bringing sweets and pressed
flowers secured between small
panes of glass, sealed with wax
at the edge so she might bring
a piece of the sun's own creation
down below, a memento of our time
in the summer in those moments
I slipped away.

when the day came that I had to

make a choice between the embrace
of the day and the cool waters of
night, I knew that deep down
I just wanted to be warm.

somehow I felt myself sinking
with cold hands pressed against
my hot cheeks.

*if I told her how much I wanted her
to hold my hand and never let it go*

*if I told her how much I wanted to feel
her naked pulse against mine*

*if I told her she would be the reason
I loved daylight and the moon above
and the summer's breeze*

*if I told her she would be the reason
I dreamt of winter in a little house
by the woods where the snow would
sparkle like diamonds in the midnight sky*

*if I told her that she had stolen my heart
a thousand times before
then maybe she would not have to steal
it again in every
incarnation*

Forget

when I am too still and let the wind
settle so no music comes from the
ever-speaking trees or the twinkling
bells in the meadow, I can hear faint
ringing and vibration

but these foreign sounds only make me
summon up the chorus, orchestrate
the loudest drums and the rushing
of the creek too frantic for its true
gentle passage

I bury deep those hateful sounds,
dilute them with the thunder of my
nature, staving off reminders of a
disconnected time where I was not
the master of my own road

A Prayer

maybe it's the moon
or the peace of this spot
and my ignorance
of the hardness of nature
or the blood slowly beading
on my tired skin

I don't know
and I do not care
but I was grateful
to be here
at all

Is She...?

I had been taught about the cells
atoms and proteins that made me
up. I knew the general idea.

and so
when I sat holding her hand, listening
to the songs she loved but I never
knew, I examined her skin
turning over her palms like book pages
looking for answers to questions I was
only starting to ask again. like maybe if
I was perfectly still I could crane
my eyes to see whether it was
even possible that she was made
from the same stuff as
me, capable of things like
leaving invisible wounds in
invisible places.

I thought maybe that stillness
could let my eyes move carefully
like an owl among starlings, then
I could see beneath her body
that beautiful shiny blue
but no matter how hard I looked
I never found it.

I was glad I never found

anything I was looking for
and gave up the hunt,
stopped manifesting the beast
under her flesh.

never again gave a shit
whether or not she was made
of the same stuff as
me.

some nights I could
hear the stones
I'd buried in the closet
screaming out

carry me carry me carry me

you must you must you must

it has to be you

Return

just when the daffodils started to turn
their pleasant faces up towards the morning
sun I heard the creak of wheels coming
up the path and rushed out. it could only mean
she was returning, back with her trunk
filled with the prizes of her journey.

I ran out to meet her with a joyful
shout, nearly knocking her off her feet
with my greeting. the road had gone on
for long miles of solitude, but in time
the daffodils came along to signal she
was close, and delighted her with
their dainty glory.

dear one she whispered
as we turned our backs to the yellow
sentinels, *they're so beautiful*

I made them all for you, I preened
trying to enchant the world
around us so she would never
again be tempted to leave for
days on end. *so you would remember
how to find your way home.*

and then it was like she had never
left at all, save for the words hanging

in the air: *my dear, to the end*
I will remember your daffodils
sweetest things of all.

Ungrateful

little cat buried
somewhere inside the ball
of fur, tightly wound
in a sunbeam
on a cushion
on a bench

careful!
the charming cat
is stretching on the bed
as if it's dancing

creamed or navy with
beige and pink

chew-chewing, paws
drumming, eyes
closed.

is it sly and
does it catch fish?
picking them up
showing them to me

a charming cat does not
appear to spend
a moment worrying
about its dinner

but smiling it shows me
how my poor cooking
comes up short

I Am So Afraid

I am afraid to call it a
daydream, more meaningless
word than dream

a place with less time
less substance
less memory
lingering on the skin
for days after.

for now
it's real and the half-filled
glass of lemonade
sitting on the wooden table
with a book left open
on a page doubtless
with something exceptionally
beautiful written on it
will taste as sweet
and as sour
as I expect.

Devotion

little notes tucked into my pocket
are a thing to anticipate every
time I head out the door, bag over
my shoulder, axe in hand
setting off to do the day's work
collect mushrooms
fix the neighbour's bridge
sell her weavings or biscuits
in the village.

once outside the garden gate
I already press a hand against
the breast pocket of my coat
to feel the promised crinkle
of paper. sweet words
I will savour like candy
later in the day.

when the evening draws in
I will drag the table close
to my chair
light a lamp
enjoy the autumnal shadows
of the trees
of the valley

but by then the paper will be
squashed, it will be worn

its grey cover discoloured
and fine scent long gone
gathering dust

but if I do pull it out
 a cloud of blue air
will gather in the room, like a
soft wind from an open window
I will open my eyes and
stare at the poem
intently

is it good
this time?

the poem, a day old
is small but possesses
an emotional depth
that shines through

and the act of reading it
in the quiet of the evening
will fill me with emotion

and it will become a part of me
as all words do.
this will become true until
the day when I turn
the last page
and close the book.

Rot

how did it get to this? how did
longing and displacement in
an unfamiliar home
send me to another world

at least I must assume
I am far from those unloved places
because how could this
this woman
this life
exist there?

I think it over with a mixed
heart, picking apples from gnarled
trees, their chaotic branches
forming a perfect ladder for my
sojourn.

*(you're not the only one
who's longing, you know)*

there is peace in these leaves and
in my hands; one gathers and the
other rejects. I bring them home
to add to the heap of the
precious.

no matter where I was before

when I am in these treetops I feel
safe, and in this apple patch I am
present. I notice the many
strange endless beautiful shades
of life as I stand on my own
two feet.

I wonder if galatea
feared aphrodite,
longing to stay
marble.

Tracks

on the days I don't let it
get to me, when I pack those
worries up in a tightly tied bundle
and bury them like nightclothes
under the bed covers, we go to
the racetrack.

something I might have laughed
at before, but it seems so pleasant
and diverting when it comes with her
in that dress, the basket filled with
cream and scones, flasks of tea and
cherries and honeyed plumbs, the small
brown paper bags with brown paper
wrapping. all clean and tidy like
something from a magazine.

we sit in the small seats by the rail
looking out at the track, at the fields beyond
not looking at each other for once. my eyes
drift to the horses and their trunks
and legs and feet, waiting to pull
away from the gates, leaving and entering
the races.

afterwards we sit there on the cool grass
and she pushes a couple of the scones
aside to get my attention with her legs

and her voice.

she begins talking about horses
the pedigrees and the bloodlines
not about sex and fillies and colts
but about the subtle differences
between the various breeds

how they were bred for strength
and stamina. she talks about the
trainers and the owners and the pre-race
rituals and the jockeys.

how the jockeys feel the weight and
the power and the strength of the
horses while they are waiting for the
gates to swing and close

about the prep they do to make them
ready for the races. how the jockeys brush
and brush and groom the horses
even putting their nose to the animal's
pasterns to feel their feet (I can't
believe in such levels of trust)

she talks about drying the manes, about
oiling and the conditioners and the shine
and the felt of the feet, the legs and
about the scratches the horses get
from the dirt and the mud
and from the jockeys running into each other
but not caring.
not really.

just as long as the race is run
and the horse is finished
so they won't have to stop and tend
the wounds.

then she talks about the well-fed and
the cold-stiffened trainer and the racing
schedule, about betting and wagering,
about sitting in the box and what
winning and losing stands for.

she talks about the strategy
about what each horse needs to do
to win. as if there was something buried
in this encyclopedic knowledge that
is meant to be instructive.

as if I might know or understand it.
and I won't, not as she does.

she doesn't expect me to understand
and doesn't tell me that I have the right
to know. but I wish I did. I wish I did
because it would make her seem more
human, more relatable, more like the
rest of us with the same problems.

at least I would feel as though I understood
instead of caught in these secret circles
that we call lives

Evolve

nothing may stay the same

not the river nor the skies

far harder things to alter

than the tender flesh

of the heart

Medicine

in a moment of panic
I rushed to the cupboard
and knocked over jars
and bottles, seeking the
one I always mislaid
or perhaps the one that
was always escaping
labeled medicine.
it became harder and
harder to find each time
it ran away.

I tried different hiding-holes
elbow-deep in the cupboard
or wedged in a crevice
or still safe lying beneath our
mattress. it escaped through
cracks and fissures
into unlikely places, so mysterious
that there was no map
anywhere to take me
to it.

then the next day, a holiday
it finally popped out
from the big grey cupboard
and went running around
in circles, a dervish dancing.

*this thing has me in a mess
and I don't know what to do,*
I said to my wife. *just like
the snake that came in
through the door and had us
locked inside our room
all night long.*

luckily, she only
laughed, patted my hand
and left me to fight my battle
of the bottle and the dishes.

I left the medicine to its tantrum
and went to pick up the
teapot. it felt perfectly
ordinary. I reached to turn
the handle, with all its notches
and cracks, worn porcelain
chipped foot crusted with time.

it had a new lid, and fit
perfectly right in its
cupboard where it was
supposed to be.

it was the colour of the
sea, and if I asked my
friends they might say
it was an antique, though
I couldn't recall the last
time we spoke. anyway
they could never understand

the crazy old woman who
would spend hours arguing
about teapots and bottles
whether they were new or
even belonged to us
at all.

as I stood there after
pouring in the water, all the
feelings it was supposed to
stir – nostalgia, comfort,
home – were missing. I knew
that in one way I was more
broken than I started. I had
been sorting out my life
on the outside, but hadn't
really sorted out my porcelain
interior and was making messes
as usual.

a teapot and tea-maker.
how to love and respect both
at the same time,
or something like that.

Unbutton

she traced the lines
that ran down my shoulder
the image of a ship
that was meant to remind
me of something
(she makes me forget what)
and asked me about the time
before her. questions I'd begged
a reprieve from many
times.

the churn of my stomach
uncertain sea
made me hesitate;
to tell or remember?
I wasn't sure, but
this time I tried
anyway.

I told her about the time
I made the radio, and
the time I bought the records
and the first time I was beaten
and the time I was
arrested.

she rolled her eyes, shook
her head. I heard her mutter

something about poor kids
who lived in the streets and
couldn't afford to buy records
or make radios.

she reached across the
table and touched my hand
saying we'd all made so many
mistakes, but that our mistakes
hadn't changed who we were
or what mattered most about
our souls, or our spirits maybe
maybe not, but in the long run
those were the things that
mattered.

and I knew then
that she was right
about who I was
and why I mattered

but I tried to keep my
revelation almost
inaudible. I wanted her
to be the one to say it
out loud.

she asked
if that was all I had
to say and I just
nodded.

she patted my hand, stood

and looked up at the sky
pulled me close, kissed me
and then walked off
into the night.

I longed to walk
away too, but I was scared
of what would come out
from under me
the moment I stood
to rise.

I called after her
called her name again
and again but I couldn't
make her
reappear.

Cracked Foundation

the ground pounced in
catching me unawares
a roiling earthquake meant
not to destroy, but to
unsettle.

how can the sunlight feel
so soft on my skin
when everything else
threatens to fall apart?

The Thinking Place

it's good to have some little space
where one can be alone; at first
it was where I went to wait, but
now it's an escape. a cobbled path
I found in the woods one summer
unused by the willow-wacks
straggling silver grass nipping
at naked ankles.

here is the house
of the court of birds, the chattering
circle like a hive, rounds of branches
housing plumed ministers. I fix
my cuffs and enter the fray.

their counsel is a comfort for
our languages are not the same
they don't care for my little troubles
only that my coos are no longer
in harmony. when I sink
a little, their great ruffling urges
me back up.

today the brush-brush and
the flit-flit is loud.

I have learned three lessons
from my unwitting teachers

in the time I've been under
their tutelage:

bear no gifts
for when I brought
foolish pockets of seed
I nearly lost both eyes
without thanks

tell no lies
as I couldn't return for
weeks after thinking
perhaps I could fashion myself
the wings they wore so proudly

and leave nothing unsaid
for with every turn of the season
we never know which voice
will be gone
from the chorus

today I bring my case to them
am I imagining this or
with seedless pockets and
wingless back and
nothing that I'm not
willing to say.

am I imagining this or
is something changing?

The Long Sentence

somehow I'm finding myself in the role
of cleaning up the mess: the thread
trimmings cling to the rug under
the carpet after her weaving is done.

my heart my arms
rung with yarn, needles, raw silk.
sympathy coils around my wrist
the harmless garden snake
that I would love to find at the end
of every slithering tail

but no matter: I will clean
in steady tribute to the mistake
I once made (long forgotten).
I will clean because once upon
a time I hurt somebody
and will spend every day
refusing forgiveness and
amends.

Awakening

I asked her if
the leaves knew how
to fall here. she
laughed, not feeling
the winter that was
threatening
inside me.

I saw her face
predicted in the blackness
of night, the reflection
of sun on ice, a floe

she walked towards me
laying a kiss on my
forehead, my lips. *the
leaves know
how to fall here.*

she smiled
and my pulse
pumped.

Indentured

the invitation lay on the
table in the hall for a day
as was proper
before she sent me out
to return it, signed and
sealed. accepting the request
that we join company to
celebrate the bliss of
another couple.

it seemed a normal thing
as we selected flowers for
our crowns and satins for
our skirts. though strange
to conjure such an occasion
given my dislike of formality
and our own disregard
for ceremonial bond

but I was becoming more
like a rock on the river
bank, made smooth
by constant repetition
and pushing, though the
friction was as gentle as
a kiss.

we entered the hall, stargazer

paradise, pressed and scented
with jasmine. only then I realized
that I was a shadow behind
her regal form, that I was the
plus-one; for it was no invitation
but a request
for a blessing.

she walked with purpose
down the aisle, towards the happy
couple, some shapes meant
to represent something but
I was far too taken by
the throne on the altar
as blooming as the garden
beneath our bedroom
window. she found her
seat there, her eyes
not catching mine, but a
finger meant to beckon.

I walked the aisle too
puzzling whether this
was some sort of sabotage,
some kind of metaphor,
something meant to show
me a lesson, but all
I was learning was
the fear that strikes a rabbit
when the meadow goes
too still.

the motions came to me

like a spell. I bowed, hands
on my hips, prostrated face
like a nude statue of an Oread
begging with my gaze for
explanation.

I might have embarrassed her
for she laughed. *just you and me
my love. we will both make
our presence felt.*

I nodded, unsure whether
this was something to be
grateful for; at least I was not
banished from this strange
game of kingdoms. with a
decision to smile I paid
respect to my queen's throne.

this done, she brushed me
aside to carry on with the
ceremony. I found some perch
beside her, but struggled
to look at the faceless folk
who held her in such
reverence. I looked down
at my chest through the
tulle and lace. was not
the map burned into
my skin?

*we are grateful for
your blessing* said the

bride, kneeling in
the aisle. *we will hold
no gift more dearly.*

my queen raised a
languid hand: *the eyes
of a dog will maintain
their stare through the
window, longing as they
cannot hear the crack
of the whip on the
other side*

some blessing.
I placed my hands before
my jester's mouth and
uttered with a shaky breath
*you might have better business
offering a palm of kindness to
the others in your kingdom
who are to be your subjects
in this transition*

it's an ego thing,
she said.

later, we were again alone
in the forest. the sun was almost
set, the very heavens screaming
for attention with wails of orange
and pink. I had no idea
why we'd come here.
I'd watched her leave the throne

room, walked down the rampart,
unable to hear the queen's thoughts
and wondering why.

there, among the birch
for the very first time
we looked at one another. I was
a bear, she a cub, my paws
like her paws. but hers was the
twin gaze of a snake.

my queen my queen
why must you tempt
and have me obey you
just to stand here in the dark?
I'm not asking for much
just transform me
bring me back to life
I beg you to
bring me back to life.

the forest was all the more
darker for the shift as I felt
as if I had stayed too long
in some place that turned
dangerous after nightfall

oh darling she said
her eyes roaming from me
what's so wrong about
me not transforming you
just yet? let's just agree
that I will. after all, we both

want the same thing. I'm talking
of freeing you from all the burdens
to finally make you feel
as free as you deserve.
why do you insist on the
forbidden fruit? what if
you've really been living your
life wrong? I am just the next
step, and you'll need my help
to get there.

she did not let her voice rise
above a gentle whisper. for a
moment I felt we were one, then
heard a rustle in the bushes
and drew back.

I could not see the snake now
but I did see the opening
it was gone but I knew
it would be back.

there is a god
who does not make friends
but courts those who long
without knowing
what for.

Withdrawals

what kind of flower
do you want today? I asked
pulling my rested and aching
body up into the day, leaving
behind mussed blankets where
she still laid half in sleep.
her hair sprung out from
around her face as if
in celebration of finding
another morning. she raised
a hand and I wondered what
it was meant to communicate
as I stumbled into trousers.
she insisted on starting each
day with my calloused hands
gently parting and weaving her
long hair into a fine and orderly
coil marked with flowers still
trembling with dew plucked
only minutes before she
rose.

later, with heavy steps
she'd make her way down
the stairs to our front door
followed by an echo
of all the times I had
called to her,

still calling out into
the day so the sun might shine
for both of us. how my
heart would beat against
my chest as I followed
behind.

  sometimes she'd let me catch
    up. other times it took all my
      strength not to fall behind
        my own feet leading me down
        the street which ran parallel to
        the choking gardens of flowers
       and sunlight. I saw a neighbour
       out tending her lawn, and bent to
      pick a blossom for my love. she
     understood as I held the flower
    to my nose, my breath
burnt with the scent.

but she didn't notice the flowers
in the wide white street as I chased
after her. I wanted to tell her to stop
and look and know the difference,
so I could tell her which ones were
for her, and which ones were not but
she walked right by.

I trailed behind
I wanted to run
to join her
but my heart was
still so heavy

I could not convince
her of anything.

she wore white today, white
skirt and white top, hair cascading
as I saw her last. she turned
slowly, red eyes alight
with some confused emotion, smile
fading. she reached out her
hand as if for reassurance, as if
to tell me she would not forget.

but I was still slow
to follow. I walked, stumbled
flower in left hand
set on her side.
I held her as the sound
of her heels plunged
into the pavement.

I wanted her to want me
I wanted her to kiss me
I wanted her to touch me

but all I got was an echo

an echo of an echo
that would last
until I gave up my shadow
walking.

I held her though her
last breath, I held her

until she was dry.

then finally I put her
down, took one last gust
of air into my lungs

in the middle of the street,
I fell to my knees.
I cried until I was
done.

Exodus

no matter how delicious

the bounty of summer

still the fall must come

no matter how captivating

the world of the story

still the page must turn

Maelstrom

it felt like the world was
ending and I feared to look
out the window, for the deep
and unrelenting knowledge
that the sky had cast off
its ever-blue and swirled with
end-of-days black.

I felt it coming in my bones. of course
this would be the moment I couldn't
find her. the one time I feared
would come, when I would need her anchor
to keep me in my chosen harbour.

I could hear distant voices and see
a lidded sunlight when I blinked
my eyes. *please no, please
don't leave me
please don't take her away*

I sat for a minute, listening
not moving. the world held
its breath for the end.

*you'd do the same thing,
I bet. make a joke or a song
or a play to stop the world
from fracturing.*

Burn the Witch

I thought she was going to
die. that's how strange she looked
as I found her, the day taking another
dark turn. some strange substance
working its way into her blood, disagreeing
with her. I could have told it that was
a bad idea.

but I knew what she wanted me
to do, and took the sheet from the
clotheslines to wrap her, somehow as small
as a broken bird
and carried her into the forest. the beds
of moss parted their pine needle cloaks
to make a soft place for her to return
to me. I set her down and prayed.

the forest answered

she'd been granted a reprieve
for now. in that moment of exhaustion
she whispered in my ear the voice
of promise, and I knelt to pray more then
went back to work. the act was all
that was required, and I left her sleeping
head on chest.

it would be the middle of the night

when I'd awaken from my sleep
and see her in bed where
she belonged, eyes closed
a small smile, lips pouting. my memories
rushed back as she laid there,
so many shades of the moon.

it became clear to me then
that what I'd prayed for was
granted. I was not as powerless
as I had assumed.

but my head was still foggy
with visions, hard to parse.
I couldn't understand how such
a tragedy had befallen a girl so
unlike me, but so much like the
person I've found myself becoming
lately.

in the empty times, it would have
seemed cruel.
but I knew in my heart
that I was in danger.

I was bound by the string between us
that gave me power
I'd never used it yet, but made
the decision to use it
then.

I knew that once the act
was done, the tether was gone.

what would I do? I pulled a broad
face out of my memory, a face
I thought I'd invented.
the fire began to dance.
I had to do something.

somewhere deep in my core
I felt that fire being born, saw
that it was not something I had
to extinguish

it had purpose
it had energy
it burned in the open air
it kept me young

as I left her to sleep with
her dress soaked in the blood
it was time

I put out the light
and with the fire
the way was bright

it would take
I just knew it would
I lit the pile of wood
that burned to feed
the flames
I don't know why this
was important to me

I began the laborious task

of ripping the cloth off the
thing that had been her.
I'd made a conscious decision
that she would not go gently,
for there is little tenderness in
the act of skinning the beast.

not working fast enough
with the dress off, I dropped
to my knees, touched her hair,
blood running hot, out of
control blinding, and suddenly
I wasn't ready
to let her go

but she said something
to me, in my mind – I don't
know how. she could no longer
speak. my heart broke
but I kept working until
finally I watched the flame
eat her,
watched the flame
watched the flame
and saw

I saw the flame go out
and I knew
that no fire ever
comes back to life.

the last words I heard
on the air were *let's be free*

*our time is almost up
you are the master*

I've since wondered what
it all meant. her acts of treason
in seeing an opportunity and
taking it. not that I would have
done differently: I cannot fault
my beast for making a
frankenstein of me

*I hope you find it in yourself
to free yourself*

I wanted to control her, own
her reactions to the kind of love
I had to offer. a sad little play
that any critic would pick apart
and she offered a mercy
in changing the script. it shone
harsh light: maybe this genre
isn't for you. maybe I needed to
abandon the pen, the letter, the
need to spill words and just feel
the fire, react to the heat. feel
the stone weights and build
stronger muscles. read the map
and book the flight instead
of making endless expanding
wishlists. listen for the click
as the manacles fall
to the ground.

I heard a whisper,
always present
if only I'd known what
to listen for all along.

*don't be bound
by the string.*

she said
*but remember
I love you*

she said
*let's be free
our time is almost up
you are the master.*

What Happens Next

she was gone.

and all the spaces she once filled were blank white
it took more strength than I knew
flowed under my skin
to find something beautiful
to put into those lonely places
but I had to believe that eventually
those rough edges would start to
turn smooth.

Pocket

I had to figure out the quicksand
lesson. tore my shirt to see the map,
knowing from a lifetime of sidelining
that what came next was crucial. I ran
back to the cottage, into the cupboard
to find the stones: my pockets
hungry and ready for their steady
burden. the anchors I'd been
needing. I dug deep into my
memories: the horses on the track
pink bottles with green stems inside
gingham on soft grass, hands
warm and pressing on tender things.
where was the key? what would finally
turn the latch? I ran into the wild,
the place of endless pathways.

the trees had dressed for grieving,
all in white. blankets for slumber.

I held my breath in that winter
snow for clues, but all I could hear was
mmmmm... not-mmmmmm... rrr-rrrrrr-rrr-rrrrr-rrr
stumbling onto a track, the sound
father down, maybe fifty yards
off I heard it again: not-mmmmm. rrr-rrr-rrrrr.

it was so close, I was sure it had

to be a train. there had to be one. I needed
an exit, and fast.

I just had
to find the station.
a station where the
next part of everything
would begin.

it just had to be
early. just around the next curve,
again: not-mmmmm....
not-mmm. rrr-rrr-rrr-rrrrr-rrr.

what was that? I was sure it must be
for me. some distant beeping
growing closer. not-mmm.
rrr-rrr-rrr-rrrrr-rrrrr.

with every step I took down the track,
it grew louder. I ran for it,
pockets thundering against thighs,
needing it
to take me back
to the place that comes alive
when the lights come on and
the curtains are raised
for the dawn.

I am ready
to live again

Renewal Season

I give her all the credit. she was
a powerful enchantress, a wise
and cunning fox, a queen
in a story without a hero. I gave her
leave to be everything I did not think
I could be, everything I thought
I did not need or deserve
to feel. but when the mirror broke
on cold steel, alarmed voices and
electronics, there was only one truth
left in the wake of the dark.

I am a builder. I craft lives
in fine and slender timber
supple but strong. it was only I who
did not see the power of two hands
and of a choice to accept
the freedom I had not claimed.
I did not realize that my art
was not confined to the realm
of dreams.

as you may have heard, I am now
the ruler of a new kingdom, empire
for the noble and the brave. I decided
to live and let live. I built with some prudence,
a design that could withstand and hide.
a fortress so high that my enemies

could not stand the heights, and would not
wish to stand against the world's champion
of ladders.

I planted the seed of it
it in the dark and chose
a time when the rest of the world slept,
a time when no one would be stirring.

I turned away from fruitless
attempts at rewriting the past
to simply make amends
and move on, no longer
looking back.

I have forsaken many things, and walk
an uncertain path, but I have found the heart
of the matter:

I am woman.

bit by bit I build the world.

every day and if
it is mighty g[ood]
that this is to [be]
the last time [I]
have to put [in]
the days witho[ut]
you dearest. I [don't]
want to go to sh[ow]
anything, all [I]
want is my ow[n]
girl. Everything
enters around

About the Author

Riva Wilson is a writer and artist from Nova Scotia, Canada. With a background deeply rooted in Classics and fantasy literature, she strives to create literary worlds like rich tapestries with enough detail to keep you busy for hours. She also composes music and loves to travel the world, gathering inspiration and creative material.

Also publishing under R.E. Wilson for fiction, and Rebecca Wilson for non-fiction.

Instagram: @artifactualist
Website: artifactualist.com

Other Works

By Riva Wilson:

Hunter of Buried Things (March 2022)

By R.E. Wilson:

The Night Wheel
Joseph Darby: A Man of Sable Island
The Ancient Frankenstein

www.ingramcontent.com/pod-product-compliance
Lightning Source LLC
Chambersburg PA
CBHW070046120526
44589CB00035B/2354